A Different Drummer

D1712747

Leroy L. Prendhomme

A DIFFERENT DRUMMER

Being Free,

Being with Nature,

Being Yourself…

in the words of Henry David Thoreau

Selected by Kermit Farnsworth

A DIFFERENT DRUMMER

*These are true mornings
        of creation,
original and poetic days,
not mere repetitions of the past.
There is no lingering
of yesterday's fogs,
only such a mist as might have
adorned the first morning.*

Journal, January 6, 1858

Let me live where I will, on this side is the city, on that the wilderness, and ever I am leaving the city more and more and withdrawing into the wilderness. I should not lay so much stress on this fact if I did not believe that something like this is the prevailing tendency of my countrymen. I must walk toward Oregon. . . .

From "Walking"

Plainly the fox belongs to a different order of things from that which reigns in the village. Our courts, though they offer a bounty for his hide, and our pulpits, though they draw many a moral from his cunning, are in few senses contemporary with his free forest life.

Journal, 1837-47

As I come over the hill, I hear the wood thrush singing his evening lay. This is the only bird whose note affects me like music, affects the flow and tenor of my thoughts, my fancy and imagination. It lifts and exhilarates me. It is inspiring. It is a medicative draught to my soul. It is an elixir to my eyes and a fountain of youth to all my senses. It changes all hours to an eternal morning. It banishes all trivialness. It reinstates me in my dominion, makes me the lord of creation. . . .

Journal, June 22, 1853

It is true, I never assisted the sun materially in his rising; but, doubt not, it was of the last importance only to be present at it.

From *WALDEN*

I'll walk with gentle pace,
And choose the smoothest place,
And careful dip the oar,
And shun the winding shore,
And gently steer my boat
Where water-lilies float,
　　And cardinal flowers
Stand in their sylvan bowers.

From TO THE MAIDEN IN THE EAST

Remember thy creator in the days of thy youth. Rise free from care before the dawn, and seek adventures. Let the noon find thee by other lakes, and the night overtake thee everywhere at home. There are no larger fields than these, no worthier games than may here by played. Grow wild according to thy nature, like these sedges and brakes. . . . Let not to get a living be thy trade, but thy sport. Enjoy the land, but own it not. Through want of enterprise and faith men are where they are, buying and selling, and spending their lives like serfs.

From *WALDEN*

Our life is frittered away by detail. . . . Simplify, simplify.

From *WALDEN*

*I*n my boating of late I have several times scared up a couple of summer ducks of this year, bred in our meadows. They allowed me to come quite near, and helped to people the river. I have not seen them for some days. Would you know the end of our intercourse? Goodwin shot them, and Mrs. _____, who never sailed on the river, ate them. Of course, she knows not what she did. What if I should eat her canary? Thus we share each other's sins as well as burdens. The lady who watches admiringly the matador shares his deed. They belonged to me, as much as to any one, when they were alive, but it is considered of more importance that Mrs. _____ should taste the flavor of them dead than that I should enjoy the beauty of them alive.

Journal, August 16, 1858

Kathe Hamilton

I was reminded, this morning before I rose, of those undescribed ambrosial mornings of summer which I can remember, when a thousand birds were heard gently twittering and ushering in the light.... The serenity, the infinite promise, of such a morning! The song or twitter of birds drips from the leaves like dew. Then there was something divine and immortal in our life, when I have waked up on my couch in the woods and seen the day dawning, and heard the twittering of the birds.

Journal, March 10, 1852

I hear faintly the cawing of a crow far, far away, echoing from some unseen wood-side, as if deadened by the springlike vapor which the sun is drawing from the ground. It mingles with the slight murmur of the village, the sound of children at play, as one stream empties gently into another, and the wild and tame are one. What a delicious sound! It is not merely crow calling to crow, for it speaks to me too. I am part of one great creature with him.

Journal, January 12, 1855

*T*ime is but the stream I go a-fishing in. I drink at it; but while I drink I see the sandy bottom and detect how shallow it is. Its thin current slides away, but eternity remains.

From *WALDEN*

There are from time to time mornings, both in summer and in winter, when especially the world seems to begin anew, beyond which memory need not go, for not behind them is yesterday and our past life; when, as in the morning of a hoar frost, there are visible the effects as of a certain creative energy, the world has visibly been recreated in the night. Mornings of creation, I call them....It is the poet's hour. Mornings when men are new-born, men who have the seeds of life in them.

Journal, January 26, 1853

For many years I was self-appointed inspector of snow-storms and rain-storms, and did my duty faithfully.

From *WALDEN*

*T*here was a time when the beauty and the music were all within, and I sat and listened to my thoughts, and there was a song in them. I sat for hours on rocks and wrestled with the melody which possessed me. I sat and listened by the hour to a positive though faint and distant music, not sung by any bird, nor vibrating any earthly harp. When you walked with a joy which knew not its own origin. When you were an organ of which the world was but one poor broken pipe. I lay long on the rocks, foundered like a harp on the sea-shore, that knows not how it is dealt with. You sat on the earth as on a raft, listening to music that was not of the earth, but which ruled and arranged it. Man *should be* the harp articulate.

Journal, May 23, 1854

I know of but one or two persons with whom I can afford to walk. With most the walk degenerates into a more vigorous use of your legs, ludicrously purposeless, while you are discussing some mighty argument, each one having his say, spoiling each other's day, worrying one another with conversation, hustling one another with our conversation. I know of no use in the walking part in this case, except that we may seem to be getting on together towards some goal; but of course we keep our original distance all the way. Jumping every wall and ditch with vigor in the vain hope of shaking your companion off. Trying to kill two birds with one stone, though they sit at opposite points of compass, to see nature and do the honors to one who does not.

Journal, November 8, 1858

Leroy L. Prendhomme

I long for wildness, a nature which I cannot put my foot through, woods where the wood thrush forever sings, where the hours are early morning ones, and there is dew on the grass, and the day is forever unproved. . . .

Journal, June 22, 1853

*T*hrough our own recovered innocence we discern the innocence of our neighbors.

From *WALDEN*

*S*trange that so few ever come to the woods to see how the pine lives and grows and spires, lifting its evergreen arms to the light, — to see its perfect success. . . .

From *THE MAINE WOODS*

*I*t has come to this, — that the lover of art is one, and the lover of nature another, though true art is but the expression of our love of nature. It is monstrous when one cares but little about trees and much about Corinthian columns, and yet this is exceedingly common.

Journal, October 9, 1857

A windy day. . . . Ah, if I could put into words that music which I hear; that music which can bring tears to the eyes of marble statues! — to which the very muscles of men are obedient!

Journal, September 28, 1852

*T*he blue-bird carries the sky on his back.

Journal, April 3, 1852

James Fromme

I never found the companion
that was so companionable
as solitude.
We are for the most part more lonely
when we go abroad among men
than when we stay
in our chambers.
A man thinking or working
is always alone,
let him be where he will.

From *WALDEN*

*A*lone in distant woods or fields, in unpretending sproutlands or pastures tracked by rabbits, even in a bleak and, to most, cheerless day, like this, when a villager would be thinking of his inn, I come to myself, I once more feel myself grandly related, and that cold and solitude are friends of mine. I suppose that this value, in my case, is equivalent to what others get by church-going and prayer. I come to my solitary woodland walk as the homesick go home. I thus dispose of the superfluous and see things as they are, grand and beautiful. I have told many that I walk every day about half the daylight, but I think they do not believe it. I wish to get the Concord, the Massachusetts, the America, out of my head and be sane a part of every day. . . . I wish to know something; I wish to be made better. I wish to forget, a

considerable part of every day, all mean, nar-
row, trivial men, ... and therefore I come out
to these solitudes, where the problem of existence is simplified. I get away a mile or two
from the town into the stillness and solitude
of nature, with rocks, trees, weeds, snow about
me. I enter some glade in the woods, perchance,
where a few weeds and dry leaves alone lift
themselves above the surface of the snow, and
it is as if I had come to an open window. I see
out and around myself.... This stillness, solitude, wildness of nature is a kind of thorough-
wort, or boneset, to my intellect. This is what
I go out to seek. It is as if I always met in those
places some grand, serene, immortal, infinitely
encouraging, though invisible, companion, and
walked with him.

Journal, January 7, 1857

Mike McClue

There seem to be two sides of this world, presented us at different times, as we see things in growth or dissolution, in life or death. For seen with the eye of the poet, as God sees them, all things are alive and beautiful; but seen with the historical eye, or eye of the memory, they are dead and offensive. If we see Nature as pausing, immediately all mortifies and decays; but seen as progressing, she is beautiful.

Journal, March 13, 1842

I went to the woods because I wished to live deliberately, to front only the essential facts of life, and see if I could not learn what it had to teach, and not, when I came to die, discover that I had not lived.

From *WALDEN*

I want to go soon and live away by the pond, where I shall hear only the wind whispering among the reeds. It will be success if I shall have left myself behind. But my friends ask what I will do when I get there. Will it not be employment enough to watch the progress of the seasons?

Journal, December 24, 1841

*G*ive me the poverty that enjoys true wealth.

From *WALDEN*

*T*he light which puts out our eyes is darkness to us. Only that day dawns to which we are awake. There is more day to dawn. The sun is but a morning star.

From *WALDEN*

The youth gets together his materials to build a bridge to the moon, or, perchance, a palace or temple on the earth, and, at length, the middle-aged man concludes to build a woodshed with them.

Journal, July 14, 1852

The thin snow now driving from the north and lodging on my coat consists of those beautiful star crystals. . . . How full of the creative genius is the air in which these are generated! I should hardly admire more if real stars fell and lodged on my coat. Nature is full of genius, full of the divinity; so that not a snowflake escapes its fashioning hand. . . . The same law that shapes the earth-star shapes the snow-star. . . .

Journal, January 5, 1856

I am disturbed by the sound of my steps on the frozen ground. I wish to hear the silence of the night, for the silence is something positive and to be heard. I cannot walk with my ears covered. I must stand still and listen with open ears, far from the noises of the village, that the night may make its impression on me. A fertile and eloquent silence. Sometimes the silence is merely negative, an arid and barren waste in which I shudder, where no ambrosia grows. I must hear the whispering of a myriad voices. Silence alone is worthy to be heard. Silence is of various depths and fertility, like soil. Now it is a mere Sahara, where men perish of hunger and thirst, now a fertile bottom, or prairie, of the West. As I leave the village, drawing nearer to the woods, I listen from time to time to hear the hounds of Silence baying at the Moon, — to know if they are on the track of any game. If there's no Diana in the night, what is it worth? . . . The silence was audible. I heard the unspeakable.

Journal, January 21, 1853

MEN SAY
THEY KNOW MANY THINGS

Men say they know many things;
But lo! they have taken wings, —
The arts and sciences,
And a thousand appliances;
The wind that blows
Is all that any body knows.

Each new year is a surprise to us. We find that we had virtually forgotten the note of each bird, and when we hear it again it is remembered like a dream, reminding us of a previous state of existence.... The voice of nature is always encouraging.

Journal, March 18, 1858

Most of the luxuries, and many of the so-called comforts, of life are not only not indispensable, but positive hindrances to the elevation of mankind.

From *WALDEN*

Beware of all enterprises that require new clothes.

From *WALDEN*

All our lives want a suitable background. . . . Character always secures for itself this advantage, and is thus distinct and unrelated to near or trivial objects whether things or persons.

From *A WEEK ON THE CONCORD AND MERRIMACK RIVERS*

Michael Fraser

The perception of beauty
is a moral test.

Journal, June 21, 1852

*T*he kings of England formerly had their forests "to hold the king's game," for sport or food, sometimes destroying villages to create or extend them; and I think that they were impelled by a true instinct. Why should not we, who have renounced the king's authority, have our national preserves, where no villages need be destroyed, in which the bear and panther, and some even of the hunter race, may still exist, and not be "civilized off the face of the earth," — our forests, not to hold the king's game merely, but to hold and preserve the king himself also, the lord of creation, — not for idle sport or food, but for inspiration and our own true recreation?

From *THE MAINE WOODS*

As if you could kill time without injuring eternity.

From *WALDEN*

All that was ripest and fairest in the wildness and the wild man is preserved and transmitted to us in the strain of the wood thrush. It is the mediator between barbarism and civilization. It is unrepentant as Greece.

Journal, June 22, 1853

While men believe in the infinite, some ponds will be thought to be bottomless.

From *WALDEN*

I will wander further from what I have called my home — to the home which is forever inviting me. In such an hour the freedom of the woods is offered me, and the birds sing my dispensation. In dreams the links of life are united: we forget that our friends are dead; we know them as of old.

Journal, May 23, 1853

I hear the dreaming frog ... and the cuckoo.

Journal, June 14, 1851

*T*he man who goes alone can start today; but he who travels with another must wait till that other is ready.

From *WALDEN*

Our thoughts and sentiments answer to the revolutions of the seasons, as two cog-wheels fit into each other. We are conversant with only one point of contact at a time, from which we receive a prompting and impulse and instantly pass to a new season or point of contact. A year is made up of a certain series and number of sensations and thoughts which have their language in nature. Now I am ice, now I am sorrel. Each experience reduces itself to a mood of the mind.

Journal, June 6, 1857

To him whose elastic and vigorous thought keeps pace with the sun, the day is a perpetual morning.

From *WALDEN*

If a man does not keep pace
with his companions,
perhaps it is because
he hears a different drummer.
Let him step to the music
which he hears, however measured
or far away.

From WALDEN

*Set in Palatino, a 20th Century typeface
with Venitian characteristics
designed by Hermann Zapf of Frankfurt.*

Printed on Copperfield Matte paper.

Designed by Nancy Haas